Sta

The Best

MW00940667

Stay In Your Lane Copyright © 2017 Charmas B. Lee

ISBN-13: 978-1548501754

ISBN-10: 1548501751

BISAC: Education / Leadership

Cover Design Samuel K. Thurman

Photo Courtesy of Brandon Hopper

Infographic Courtesy of Mike Mejia

STAY IN YOUR LANE
THE BEST LEADERS ARE THE GREATEST COACHES

"Stay in Your Lane provides a unique perspective on how effective leadership influences sports performance. Furthermore, the leadership nuggets described in *Stay in Your Lane* can provide a positive and lasting impact to our corporate culture. A must read!"
— **Joe V. Aldaz Jr.,**
Lt. Col., USAF (Ret)

CHARMAS B. LEE

FOREWORD BY Benita Fitzgerald Mosley,
CEO, Laureus Sport for Good Foundation USA
1984 Olympic Gold Medalist, 100 Meter Hurdles

TESTIMONIALS

Having advised CEOs and company C level staff for the last 40 years, those who approach managing as a coach have better success across the board in relating to their team. Coach Lee is spot-on in identifying the rewards of good coaching and gives excellent ways to implement better business leadership qualities. This book should be a "must read" for anyone who has the responsibility of leading; in a business, family, church, non-profits, or subordinates at work. We all must continually evaluate our managing skills and tools in the pursuit of improving them to produce successful, happy and productive employees.

Tim Devore Inc.

Coach Lee captures the elusive essence of leadership and reminds us that leading requires action. It is not enough to think it. It is not enough to say it. Leading requires **doing** and Charmas masterfully shines a light on ordinary people doing extraordinary things. It's the doing - like writing this book - that inspires us to take action. This is a MUST READ for anyone who wants to have impact.

-Beth V. Walker, Founder
Center for College Solutions

Charmas Lee has cracked the code in defining what "Leadership" is and how to establish the kind of environment to achieve success. What I appreciated most throughout each chapter of "Stay In Your Lane" was the actionable advice given for each discussion point. The content is concise and is easy to understand whether you are an athlete, business owner, or an individual that wants to be a more effective Team Leader, Supervisor, etc.This book is a must read for Personal and Professional Development.

Sherry Pittinger, Owner/CEO
A Focused Approach Inc

Charmas writes from a place of true conviction, accented by practical points that serve as a guide for the course of life. From the Battle of the Bulge to the track and field, his stories are compelling and relevant in any leadership context. This book is written for coaches by a coach and for leaders by a leader!

Dr. Joseph Sanders Ph.D
Founder, Touchstone Leadership Academy

Stay In Your Lane provides a unique perspective on how effective leadership can positive impact and influence sports performance. Furthermore, the leadership nuggets described in Stay In Your Lane can provide a positive and lasting impact to our corporate culture. A must read.

-Joe V. Aldaz Jr., Lt. Col., USAF (Ret)

Coach Lee delivers relevant applicable insights on personal responsibility, leadership and high performance. His coaching points are no-nonsense guidance designed for immediate implementation and results.

Dr. Jeffrey L. Huisingh, Ph.D

Charmas is an extraordinary human being, coach and an inspiring leader. His unconventional approach to living life and leading others is reflected in every page of this book. Most importantly, Charmas helps others become the best version of themselves.

~ Kath Schnorr

Foreword

Acknowledgements

Introduction

What is a Coach?

The Leader's Mantra

Leader's Mission Statement

FOREWORD

Charmas Lee is a next-level coach who brings a wide breadth of knowledge and leadership skills to his athletes and clients. He certainly understands the X's and O's of sport, but more importantly, he applies that knowledge in a way that motivates and inspires others. As a coach, author, public speaker, executive coach and more, he is able to transfer his knowledge to the business world to help individuals create success for themselves and their teams. Our entire family has enjoyed working with Charmas and we have benefited from his expertise in helping elevate our children's performances on the playing field and for our own professional careers. Stay In Your Lane is a must read for any individual or organization who would like to play at the next level.

Benita Fitzgerald Mosley,
CEO, Laureus Sport for Good Foundation USA
1984 Olympic Gold Medalist, 100 hurdles

ACKNOWLEDGEMENTS

This book is dedicated to my Lord and Savior Jesus Christ, my wife Janice, my success entourage, my mom and dad, every athlete that I have ever coached and learned from, and the teachers, pastors and coaches in my life who have inspired me along the way.

INTRODUCTION

Vince Lombardi, legendary coach of the Green Bay Packers once said, "Winning becomes easy if you *stick with it* long enough." Sticking with it wasn't about simply executing the X's and O's of the game. Coach Lombardi understood that creating and maintaining a winning **environment** was equally as important as mastering the ins and outs of the game.

To be the best in the business, there must be a sense of greater expectations from everyone involved. That's the ultimate challenge of leadership.

Most of us prefer to stay in our comfort zone, avoiding the discomfort required to achieve greatness. Successful leaders fight that tendency constantly. The fight against **MEDIOCRITY** is taxing. It is even more taxing from a leadership perspective, where you can't just take care of yourself; you must inspire the ones around you to follow your example.

There are hundreds, perhaps thousands of books written on the X's and O's of leadership. However, few have been written on how you, the leader, create the "context or environment" for achieving unparalleled levels of success. The attitude of the leader affects the **atmosphere** of the office and the **atmosphere** of the office affects other intangible factors such as employee morale, organizational momentum and relationship dynamics.

Stay In Your Lane is a fresh new perspective on how leaders influence others to reach their true potential. There is an old Aramaic proverb that states "**An army of sheep lead by a lion would defeat an army of lions lead by a sheep.**"

A good leader's influence will help the team achieve its goal by outlining the requirements and motivating them to stick to the plan. Leadership is influence; nothing more, nothing less. The best leaders are great coaches. Great coaches develop "Best in Class Leaders". That's what leadership is all about. With your permission, I hope to do a little bit of coaching in this book. *Stay In Your Lane* provides

examples and stories of how the *Great Ones* set the tempo

and press the agenda by establishing an environment where

winning big becomes second nature.

~Charmas B. Lee

The Servant Leader's Mission Statement

As the servant leader, I promise to set a shining example for my employees, serving each one of them faithfully and industriously. I will use my time, talent and treasure to prepare and empower them both personally and professionally. I commit to encourage, motivate, direct, educate and influence all to develop a sense of greater expectations within themselves.

~Charmas B. Lee

The Servant Leader's Mantra

I am the decisive element in the office, workplace, community and home. It is my personal approach that creates the climate. My mood that dictates the weather. Because of my influence I can make someone else's life miserable or joyous. I can choose to be a tool of torture or an instrument of inspiration. With this much *influence* comes great responsibility. Each day I chose to lead with character, compassion and courtesy, because leaders like myself give rise to the voice of others.

~Charmas B. Lee

What is a Coach?

"One who goes before and shows the way... carrying one to places that they never could have gone on their own."

Japan:
 sensei = one who has gone farther down the path

Sanskrit:
guru = one with great knowledge and wisdom

Tibet:
lama = one with spirituality and authority to teach

Italy:
maestro = master teacher of music

France:
 tutor = private teacher

England:
guide = one who knows and shows the way

Greece:
mentor = a wise and trusted advisor

Chapter One

We Emulate Who We Admire

Stay In Your Lane
The Best Leaders are the Greatest Coaches

I never had the privilege of personally meeting Tom Landry, legendary coach of the Dallas Cowboys, but in my youth, I was afforded the opportunity to watch him just about every Sunday during football season. There were many behaviors that he demonstrated on a consistent basis that left a life-long impression with me.

Coach Laundry may, in fact, be one of the reasons I am a coach today. In a professional league led by predominately overweight coaches, *many just one cheese fry away from a major heart attack,* Coach Landry looked like he could still suit up and play. Whether the team was winning or losing he never got hijacked by emotion. I interpreted this behavior to mean that as leaders we lose our effectiveness if we are not courteous. Just as we like to be respected, we must respect others if we want them to listen to what we say. To me, Coach Landry appeared to be a humble man of quiet strength and dignity.

Stay In Your Lane
The Best Leaders are the Greatest Coaches

Coach Landry was also a man of God and that is very important to me. He was a champion both on and off the field. Finally, he was a man who not only talked-the-talk, but also walked-the-walk. If you were an athlete in the National Football League you wanted to be coached by Tom Landry.

In 1972 Coach Landry lead the Dallas Cowboys to Super Bowl Championship VI. I was only 11 years old. Watching his team win the Super Bowl reinforced three things for me. I wanted to become a great coach, role mode and leader of others. I wanted to develop champions and be a champion as well. To inspire others maintaining my appearance, health and fitness would be important.

I saw a documentary about Coach Laundry on ESPN regarding his success of over 29 years. Someone asked how he could successfully forge a team out of a group of individuals with different strengths, personalities and abilities.

Stay In Your Lane
The Best Leaders are the Greatest Coaches

Landry replied, "My job is to get men to do what they don't want to do to achieve what they always wanted to achieve."

According to George Washington Carver, "when a man does common things in an uncommon way he will command the attention of the world." As the leader, my goal is to be uncommon. I realize by making common sense a common practice in my life, I will have a positive influence on others and maybe, just maybe I will capture the attention of the world😊

Stay In Your Lane
The Best Leaders are the Greatest Coaches

Foot Stomper: Coach Landry was a champion both on and off the field.

Coaching Points

1. We emulate who we admire.

2. Be a humble person of quiet strength and dignity.

3. To inspire others my appearance, health and fitness would be important.

Stay In Your Lane
The Best Leaders are the Greatest Coaches

Chapter Two

The Power of Attitude

Stay In Your Lane

The Best Leaders are the Greatest Coaches

When I woke up this morning I dressed myself. If you are a man who has been married for at least 5 years you know how important this is... I chose my pants, my shirt, my shoes, my belt, and my sport coat. I chose my breakfast and before leaving the house I chose the attitude I would embrace for the day. I believe attitude may be the single most important performance indicator in success. Attitude is an inward feeling expressed by an external behavior. I firmly believe that it is important to develop the proper psychological and emotional attitude. Developing a winning attitude is a prerequisite to success!

Every three weeks I drive my wife Janice to an appointment in downtown Colorado Springs. We say our goodbyes and I head to the local coffee shop. On this particular day I opened the doors, walked up to the counter and order my favorite caramel caffeinated concoction; three shots of expresso, a caramel wall and the oowie gooey goodness of the specialty whipped cream!

I swipe my credit card, head down to the end of the counter and with great anticipation wait for my "little cup of heaven." A few short moments later, the barista announces in a not so friendly voice and equally poor attitude "triple con panna at the bar." "Right here" I say, smiling and raising my hand to let her know that I am at the end of the counter and ready to retrieve my drink.

The young lady deploys the drink almost spilling it on the counter, mutters a few words under her breath, turns and walks away. I take the cup to the corner table, have a seat and take a much-awaited sip. Much to my displeasure, the drink is horrible, bitter, not sweet and it smells of burnt coffee. I walk up to the counter and let the cashier know that there is something wrong with my drink. She apologizes and informs the barista to remake the espresso con panna. The barista

Stay In Your Lane
The Best Leaders are the Greatest Coaches

glances at me, rolls her eyes, lets out a sigh of aggravation and starts the process of remaking the drink.

Once the barista has completed the task, she announces "triple con panna at the bar, 2nd attempt" and places the drink on the counter very forcefully. Understanding that some days are better than others for all of us, I say thank you very much, stirring the drink as I head back to my table. Seated, with great anticipation I take a sip, expecting the smooth velvety taste of caramel and caffeine, only to be disappointed with another very, very bad con panna. Well I decided to shrug it off, thinking to myself it is only a few dollars so it's not a big deal and I discard the drink.

Three weeks pass and again it is time to drop my wife off at her downtown appointment. We say our goodbyes and I head back to the same coffee house. The same young lady is behind the bar. I walk up to the counter and asked for a triple con panna, swipe my credit card, and wait in line for my drink. A few short moments later the barista aggressively places the drink on the counter and says, "triple con panna at the bar." The gentleman next to me looks a little perplexed by the behavior, gently shrugs his shoulders and walks away. Her behavior was of no concern to me, my focus was on the beverage. "Thank you very much" I say, grab a couple of stir sticks, stir the drink, and take a sip. Sadly, it is extremely bitter without even a hint of caramel or whip cream.

This time I decide to take a different approach. Instead of going to the counter and expressing my concern, I went to the barista that made the drink. "Excuse me ma'am" I said gently, "I don't mean to be bothersome but there is something missing from this drink. I am not sure if the espresso is bad or perhaps there is not enough caramel or whip, but something is wrong!" It doesn't taste like the one they make at my home store.

Stay In Your Lane
The Best Leaders are the Greatest Coaches

She takes the drink and begins the process of remaking it. Just a few minutes later I hear the familiar words triple con panna at the bar for Lee. I pick up the drink, stir it carefully, take a sip, give the barista a thumbs-up and head to a nearby table.

Shortly afterwards the young barista comes over to my table, introduces herself and says "Sir, I am certain that I made your first drink correctly; three shots of espresso, a caramel wall and whip cream. I've made that drink several times. I guess the shots (of espresso) could have been bad, but highly doubtful."

"Well, young lady, you are the expert and if you are certain that the proper ingredients were in the drink it can only be one thing." "What's that?" she said. "It must be your attitude. *I can taste your attitude in my drink*!" The young lady was surprised with my response indicating that she never considered her attitude had such an impact on others. We had a brief, but great discussion on attitude that morning. I shared

with her how important it is to have an AM (morning) ritual so

she can show up with the best version of herself every day!

Stay In Your Lane

The Best Leaders are the Greatest Coaches

Foot Stomper: "I can taste your attitude in my drink."

Coaching Points

1. Before leaving the house, chose the attitude to embrace for the day.

2. Developing a winning attitude is a prerequisite to success.

3. Your attitude will determine how you interact with others and how others interact with you.

Chapter Three

"An army of sheep led by a lion would defeat an army of lions led by a sheep."

Old Aramaic Proverb

Stay In Your Lane

The Best Leaders are the Greatest Coaches

Great leaders possess an extraordinary sense of responsibility and dedication to their fellow human beings. The qualities and characteristics of these types of leaders inspire others to achieve beyond their goals and meet their true potential.

Most are familiar with Martin Luther King Jr. He is well known for his efforts with the civil rights movement. Another well-known humanitarian is Oskar Schindler, whose efforts to save more than 1,000 Jews were documented in Steven Spielberg's 1993 film *Schindler's List*. Both gentlemen had a deep moral conviction instilled by their faith which inspired action.

It is very unlikely that you are familiar with the name Master Sergeant Roddie Edmonds. According to history, Edmonds seemed like an ordinary American soldier but on January 27, 1945 his actions were nothing short of extraordinary.

Stay In Your Lane

The Best Leaders are the Greatest Coaches

Edmonds was captured with thousands of others in the Battle of the Bulge in late 1944. He spent 100 days in captivity. At the time of his capture most of the infamous Nazi death camps were no longer operational and many Jewish American prisoners of war were sent to a labor camp near Ziegenhain, Germany named Stalag IX-A.

This camp had a strict anti-Jew policy and segregated Jewish prisoners of war (POW'S) from the non-Jews. These camps were incredibly brutal and the chances of survival for any of its occupants was low. The American soldiers had been briefed and knew that a Jewish soldier's life would be in danger if captured, so they were told to destroy any evidence that would identify them as Jews.

On January 27, 1945, the German commander ordered all the Jews to identify themselves. Master Sergeant Edmonds knew that if they obeyed the command his Jewish comrades would be executed. Edmonds chose to disobey the order. He turned to his fellow POW's and directed everyone to step forward. Frustrated with this act of defiance the German commander turned to Master Sergeant Edmonds and said, "They cannot all be Jews." Edmonds replied, "We are all Jews here!"

Enraged, the commander pressed his pistol to Edmonds' head and offered him one last chance to obey the order. Edmonds replied with his name, rank and serial number and boldly stated "if you are going to shoot, you will have to kill us all!" With these words, the commander backed down. Per the Geneva Convention if the commander would have killed both the non-Jewish and Jewish soldiers he could have been tried for war crimes. Edmonds' action is estimated to have saved the lives of more than 200 Jewish American soldiers.

I am reminded of a quote by former President Ronald Reagan, "The character that takes command in moments of crucial choices has already been determined by a thousand other choices made earlier in the seemingly unimportant moments...It has been determined by all the day-to-day decisions made when life seemed easy and crises seemed far away--the decisions that, piece by piece, bit by bit, developed habits of discipline or of laziness; habits of self-sacrifice or self-indulgence; habits of duty and honor and integrity--or dishonor and shame."

Stay In Your Lane

The Best Leaders are the Greatest Coaches

Foot Stomper: Great leaders possess an extraordinary sense of responsibility and dedication to their fellow human beings.

Coaching Points:

1. Today, stand in the gap for one of your subordinates.

2. Character requires courage.

3. When an individual pushes his or her limits they will soon find them, however when a team pushes it's limits it can move the earth.

Chapter Four

We are Always on Audition

Stay In Your Lane
The Best Leaders are the Greatest Coaches

During a training session, I was asked an interesting question by Colin Kinsman, one of my young athletes. Colin tends to ask a lot of information seeking questions. He is seldom satisfied with a "run of the mill" response. He is intelligent and boasts a very scientific mind. Putting it mildly, Colin is an honor student and an extremely high achiever. Colin's desire and drive to excel extends itself to the track also. Colin is a senior at Woodland Park High School which is in Woodland Park, Colorado. Based on the conversations we have had, I believe that Colin will either be a politician or a scientist.

On this day Colin and I were in a deep discussion on morals, faith and ethics in business. "Coach Lee" he said, "How have you become the person that you are today? How did you arrive at this destination?" I asked Colin to give me some time to think through this question, because I wanted to answer him truthfully and would need time to process it. This question stirred my heart and affected me at a visceral level. Evidently there was something about my behavior, thoughts and actions that provoked such a question from Colin.

For the next few weeks I was caught up in the ebb and flow of life, and still was not able to give this question the time and consideration required. The depth of the question forced me to dig a little deeper and look a little further. Upon further observation, I concluded that based on the state of our world that this may be a question that should be asked of each of us to include the impoverished, the incarcerated, the affluent, those in politics, the church…all of humanity. I also believe that it begs a second question…Are you happy with the person you've become? Finally, after six weeks I befriended silence, turned my attention inward, organized my thoughts and this is the answer I provided to Colin.

I have become the person that I am today through choice, consequence and the sum-total of my experiences.

Stay In Your Lane

The Best Leaders are the Greatest Coaches

The journey that God has taken me on has been one of challenge, triumph and tragedy and with each outcome I was afforded a priceless education. I **have learned to value experiences, not things**.

During my journey, I have been treated well and have been mistreated. The lesson that I have learned from these experiences is to treat others the way that you would like to be treated, therefore I try and **treat everyone with dignity and respect**. As a coach, business owner and parent, I have learned that no two people are the same; instead we are all **equally different** therefore I applaud the commonalities that we all possess but I recognize the need to adjust for the differences as well.

I have made both good and poor choices in life, and with each choice there came a consequence. This process has taught me that I'd rather be a man of **character**, instead of being a character. I learned that it is best to be honest, sincere and authentic. No one likes a phony and it is impossible to live a life with joy if you are not the same person **within** and **without**.

I've learned that if there are twenty-five people in a room, fifteen of them may like you, five will hate you and the other five won't care. Therefore, it is important that I maintain my identity even if I am the odd man out. As a parent, coach and Christian I understand fully that I am **always on audition** and it is important to reflect Christ, after all, I may be the only Jesus someone else may ever see. I have learned to look long and hard for the good in others and to trust them until they give me a reason not to do so. It is also important not to go through life wearing rose colored glasses.

I have also learned that there is such a thing as a **healthy fear** and that **courage is not the absence of fear, it is being afraid and moving forward anyway.** I've learned that my **attitude** will determine my performance and it may be the single most important factor of all. My attitude shapes my perspective on life. Not only does it determine how I see the world; it determines how others see me.

Today I possess one of life's greatest ambitions; To create a positive change in the lives of others. As a Christian, I stand on the non-negotiable facts of my faith. My belief in Christ is the foundation of all that I am. To this there is no discussion, no negotiation, no debate. Colin, thanks for asking me the question.

Stay In Your Lane
The Best Leaders are the Greatest Coaches

Foot Stomper: "Coach Lee" he said, "How have you become the person that you are today? How did you arrive at this destination?"

Coaching Points

1. Be transparent and accessible.

2. Establish a non-intimidating, trusting environment.

3. According to Colin Powell, "When the troops stop asking you questions, you are no longer leading."

Stay In Your Lane

The Best Leaders are the Greatest Coaches

Chapter Five

Suspend Disbelief

Stay In Your Lane

The Best Leaders are the Greatest Coaches

There is an organization located in Colorado Springs, Colorado called Speed T&F. Speed T&F is a 501(c)3 non-profit track and field organization of which I am the Director of Coaching. Since its inception, Speed T&F has provided quality coaching and mentoring to thousands of student athletes in the Colorado Springs area. For 26 years this organization has consistently developed champions via the athletic arena who have become leaders that build better cultures, stronger communities, careers and outcomes. They are persistent, resilient and possess grit. They engage in positive re-appraisal and find meaning and benefit in the adversities of daily life and are likely to achieve positive outcomes. Eighty-four percent of Speed T&F athletes have received a collegiate athletic scholarship. The national average for a high school athlete receiving an athletic scholarship is a mere two percent.

Stay In Your Lane
The Best Leaders are the Greatest Coaches

This, I believe begs the question, "What makes Speed T&F successful?" Some may believe that the success of the program is reflected in the caliber of the athlete. I have been a coach for over 29 years and have helped many teams and individuals achieve unprecedented levels of success. In those 29 years I can count on one hand the number of athletes who have achieved high levels of success that possessed a unique ability, e.g., talent + ambition + predisposed genetics + higher IQ-EQ, etc. However, the majority did not possess a greater amount of talent, giftedness or skill, nonetheless went on to accomplish great things.

First and foremost, one of the primary reasons the organization has experienced extraordinary success is **connection**. We forge a link between attention and excellence. We see the personal value in each athlete and communicate and demonstrate our sincere appreciation for them in several ways. Each athlete is treated with dignity and respect. We

Stay In Your Lane
The Best Leaders are the Greatest Coaches

listen more than we speak, seeking first to understand, then to be understood. Listening is one of the best ways to demonstrate your sincere concern for someone else. Being a good listener will always lead you to the next question. Listening involves hearing what people are saying and adjusting our words and actions to response to the words and meanings we hear. This approach creates a non-intimidating environment which allows the athlete to grow mentally, physically, spiritually and academically.

According to a recent gallop poll only 30% of U.S., full-time workers are engaged at work, which means that roughly 70% of American workers aren't engaged. This may be true in the academic and athletic arenas as well. It would change the world if we all listened better. Many coaches and organizations are still using old outdated management practices which ultimately grinds the life out of them.

Stay In Your Lane
The Best Leaders are the Greatest Coaches

Secondly, we **suspend disbelief**. Athletes are trained to warm up their imaginations, give wings to their dreams and bring their athletic prowess to life. Our athletes expect the extraordinary to occur at every practice and it is amazing how the extraordinary has now become the everyday.

Stay In Your Lane

The Best Leaders are the Greatest Coaches

Foot Stomper: Listening is one of the best ways to demonstrate your sincere concern for someone else.

Coaching Points

1. Being a good listener will always lead you to the next question.

2. Forge a link between attention and excellence.

3. Suspend disbelief.

4. Expect the extraordinary daily.

Chapter Six

Burn the Boats

Stay In Your Lane

The Best Leaders are the Greatest Coaches

The standards most individuals set for themselves will usually be in a comfort zone that is well below their actual ability. If an organization is to be the best in the business, there must be a sense of greater expectations. Great leaders understand the concept of "no pressure, no diamonds." They know the key to finding the true power of the individual lies in the deep recesses of the psyche. World class leaders use emotional drivers to motivate and inspire their people to push far beyond the norm, to accomplish feats that without this level of motivation would be impossible.

As a leader, I am always looking for a competitive advantage. Those advantages may be found by studying history. One of my favorites stories is about a gentleman who dared to accomplish the impossible. He was a Spanish conquistador name Hernán Cortés. It was the year 1519 and Hernán Cortés, along with some 600 Spaniards, 16 or so horses and 11 boats, had landed on a vast inland plateau

Stay In Your Lane

The Best Leaders are the Greatest Coaches

called Mexico. The Spanish conquistador and his men were about to embark on a conquest of an empire that hoarded some of the world's greatest treasure. Gold, silver and precious Aztec jewels were just some of what this treasure had to offer anyone who succeeded in the quest to obtain it. This daring undertaking was made even more insurmountable by the fact that for more than 600 years, conquerors with far greater resources at their disposal who attempted to colonize the Yucatan Peninsula, never succeeded in doing so.

Hernán Cortés was well-aware of this fact. And it was for this reason, that he took a different approach when he arrived at the land of the Mayans. Cortez knew that before you can move people into action, you must first move them with emotion. Instead of charging through cities and forcing his men into immediate battle, Hernán Cortés stayed on the beach and awoke the souls of his men with melodious cadences – in the form of emblazoned speeches. His

Stay In Your Lane
The Best Leaders are the Greatest Coaches

speeches were ingeniously designed to urge on the spirit of adventure and invoke the thirst for lifetimes of fortune amongst his troops. His orations bore fruit, and for what was supposedly a military exploit, now bore the appearance of extravagant romance in the imaginations of Cortés' troops. As a coach, I would interpret this to be a pre-competition or mental mastery routine.

As they marched inland to face their enemies, Cortés ordered, "**Burn the boats.**" It was a decision that should have backfired. If Cortés and his men were on the brink of defeat, there wasn't an exit strategy. They were left with only two choices — die or ensure victory. Hernán Cortés became the first man in 600 years to successfully conquer Mexico. Was this act of burning the boats a mock dramatization of bravery, or a cleverly constructed strategy? History indicates that Cortés wasn't the first man to make such a bold, strategic decision to ensure victory.

Stay In Your Lane

The Best Leaders are the Greatest Coaches

In Sun Tzu's *The Art of War*, it brings to light the logic behind the decisions of history's greatest conquerors such as Alexander the Great and Taric el Tuerto, otherwise known as Tariq ibn Ziyad, the general who conquered Hispania in 711, to burn their boats at the risk of being killed in enemy hands. It was simply to **eradicate any notion of retreat** from the minds of their troops and commit themselves unwaveringly to the cause – Victory. Defeat wasn't an option.

Stay In Your Lane

The Best Leaders are the Greatest Coaches

Foot Stomper: Before you can move people into action, you must first move them with emotion.

Coaching Points

1. Burn the Boats!

2. Take a different approach.

3. Find your employee's emotional hot button.

4. Stir their imagination.

Chapter Seven

It Takes Strength to S.O.A.R.

Stay In Your Lane

The Best Leaders are the Greatest Coaches

Coaching hurdles for almost 30 years has helped me better understand how to navigate both the external and internal obstacles in life. Over the last 10 years I have had a chance to work with some of the best prep hurdlers in the country. One of the athletes achieved incredible results. As a high school senior, he won both the 110 and 300-meter hurdles at the Colorado State Track and Field Championships. He set a state record in the 300-meter hurdles that to date has not been broken. He earned the prestigious title of Colorado Gatorade Athlete of the Year. He went to Colorado State University (CSU) in Fort Collins on scholarship. Upon graduation from CSU, he had become the most celebrated athlete in school history. After his final race as a collegian he received a call from Renaldo "Skeets" Nehemiah (former Olympian who is now an agent) and was asked if he'd like to turn pro.

Stay In Your Lane

The Best Leaders are the Greatest Coaches

I share the preceding story with you because it is important to set the stage for the next athlete that I am going to introduce to you, Alexis Buckhaults. I am not certain if Alexis will become the most celebrated athlete in school history at Portland State University where she will attend on full scholarship. I don't know if when she runs her final race as a NCAA Division One athlete she will receive a call from an agent asking her if she'd like to go pro. But here is one thing for which I am certain. Alexis Buckhaults is going to change our world. In the Greek, the name Alexis means "protector or helper." I did not know this until I began my research for this story. Nonetheless based on Alexis' behaviors and actions, it is evident.

In 2014 her best performance in the 100-meter hurdles was a dismal 16.01, finishing 10th in the preliminary round of the Colorado State High School Track and Field Championships. Unfortunately for her only nine athletes advanced to the finals. In 2015 Alexis' performance improved, posting a time of 15.74. This time Alexis made the finals, finishing in 5th place overall.

Two days later Alexis joined Speed T&F for the 2015 summer program. I believe she was referred to the team by Trenton Stringari, a former high school teammate, who had been a part of Speed T&F for a couple of seasons. While in the program, Trenton had experienced a tremendous amount of success. He was also a hurdler.

My first question for Alexis was, "Why are you here?" Alexis indicated that she was dissatisfied with her previous performances over the last two years and that she wanted to be a state champion. "Alexis" I said, "Becoming a great performer (state champion) really boils down to three things; what you *really* want, what you *absolutely* believe and how *well* you prepare."

Stay In Your Lane

The Best Leaders are the Greatest Coaches

After raising six children and coaching for over 29 years I find that it is important to dig a little deeper and look a little further into a young person's response. They can say one thing, but mean something completely different. "Alexis, I really don't know what most athletes want; I only know what they say they want. Have you counted the costs, are you willing to pay the price to become the athlete you say you want to be?" "Yes, coach," she replied. "Well then, let's get to work."

And work she did. While most students were going on vacation or hanging out at the pool, Alexis was training with Speed T&F. She made the trip from Canon City, Colorado to Colorado Springs, Colorado three times a week and competed on the weekends. Within three weeks Alexis' time had improved from 15.74 to 14.89. Alexis had the fortune to be coached by three world-class coaches; Colorado Hall of Famer, Arthur "Moon" Griffin, 2000 Sydney Olympic

Stay In Your Lane
The Best Leaders are the Greatest Coaches

Paralympic Silver Medalist, John Register and myself, a Level 3 USA Track and Field Certified Coach who has met the criteria to coach at the Olympic Level.

By 2016, it was determined that for Alexis to accomplish her goal of winning a state title she must take in to account where she was willing to invest her time. Alexis was a three-sport athlete, volleyball, soccer and track and field. This left little time for off season preparation. Additionally, women's soccer and track and field run concurrently in the state of Colorado. Participating in both sports would lead to overtraining and exhaustion, which would not be part of the success formula. It truly came down to resource allocation. Alexis had to make some difficult decisions. It was possible to work around her volleyball practice and competition schedule and to improve her strength. However, to position herself for the best chance of success, she concluded that soccer would need to take a back seat.

In May of 2016, Alexis earned the title of 100-meter hurdles 4A Colorado State High School Track and Field Champion.

Photo Courtesy of Brandon Hopper

In November of 2016 Coach Register, my wife and I watched Alexis sign her national letter of intent to attend Portland State University on a full ride scholarship where she will run track and field and major in Computer Engineering and pursue a minor in Kinesiology-Biomechanics. Alexis wants to build prosthetics for Paralympic athletes and the military.

Stay In Your Lane
The Best Leaders are the Greatest Coaches

Alexis was runner-up in both the 100-meter hurdles and the triple jump at the 2017 Colorado State High School Track and Field Championships. Never being one to "settle for a lesser version of herself" she has continued training with Speed T&F in pursuit of improving her time in the 100-meter hurdles and her distance in the triple jump, to meet the qualifying standards for the Junior USA Track and Field Championships. It takes strength to soar. Alexis made a decision a long time ago to operate from the **strength** of her

highest self.

Stay In Your Lane

The Best Leaders are the Greatest Coaches

Foot Stomper: It takes strength to S.O.A.R. if you want to operate from the **strength** of your highest self and S.O.A.R. with the eagles.

Coaching Points

1. Structure your day and minimize distractions.

2. Organize your thoughts.

3. Approach every situation with a positive attitude.

4. Remain resilient even in turbulent times.

Chapter Eight

Facilitated Introspection

Stay In Your Lane
The Best Leaders are the Greatest Coaches

When I take on a new client I ask them to work on themselves for 15 minutes a day. They are asked to find one area, that if improved, would accelerate the process of becoming the person or professional that they want to be. They are instructed to write down their thoughts, comments, etc. and at the end of the week we meet for approximately 20 minutes and I ask more information seeking questions such as; Tell me more about that? What does that look like? Why is it important to you? Once I feel like I have a good understanding of the "craft", I encourage them to write a personal mission statement that is short enough to memorize. Once they have put it to memory I ask to hear it. I believe developing a powerful **mission** statement will give you **permission** to be bold and courageous!

Great leaders know that the most effective form of learning is self-discovery. Sometimes it takes facilitated introspection, asking the right questions to help people rediscover what they already know. I've learned that the best

way to predict the future is to create it yourself.

Stay In Your Lane

The Best Leaders are the Greatest Coaches

Foot Stomper: Develop a powerful **mission** statement. It will give you **permission** to be bold and courageous.

Coaching Points

1. Work on your craft for 15 minutes a day.

2. Find one area to improve to shift your trajectory in life.

3. Ask more information seeking questions.

Chapter Nine

Purpose

Stay In Your Lane

The Best Leaders are the Greatest Coaches

Most of us have heard the name Jesse Owens. Many of his accomplishments in the sport of track and field have yet to be eclipsed. Upon graduating from high school Owens attended Ohio State University. At the 1935 Big Ten Championships, within a span of 45 minutes he tied a world record in the 100-yard dash and set a long jump record of 26' 8 ¼" that would stand for 25 years. Owens also set new world marks in the 220-yard dash and in the 220-yard low hurdles.

What he is perhaps the most famous for are his efforts to support the United States Olympic team at the 1936 Berlin Olympic Games. Jesse entered the 1936 Olympics, which were held in Nazi Germany amidst the belief by Hitler that the Games would support his belief that the German "Aryan" people were the dominant race.

In all, the United States won 11 gold medals, six of them by black athletes. Owens, under extreme pressure, captured four gold medals (the 100 meters, the long jump, the

Stay In Your Lane

The Best Leaders are the Greatest Coaches

200 meters and the 400-meter relay), and broke two Olympic records along the way. This remarkable achievement stood unequaled until the 1984 Olympic Games in Los Angeles, when American Carl Lewis matched Jesse's feat. Although others have gone on to win more gold medals than Jesse, he remains the best remembered Olympic athlete because he achieved what no Olympian before or since has accomplished. During a time of deep-rooted segregation, he not only discredited Hitler's master race theory, but also affirmed that individual excellence, rather than race or national origin, distinguishes one man from another.

Jesse Owens' accomplishments both on and off the field stretch well beyond one's imagination. It's as though he was super human, or perhaps purpose drove Mr. Owens. Once an individual becomes clear on their purpose they tend to develop a powerful psychological duality and mind and body work together for a higher cause. In my profession, there

Stay In Your Lane
The Best Leaders are the Greatest Coaches

is the 5/95 rule of human performance which suggests; sport is 5 percent psychological and 95 percent physiological, however the 5 percent controls the 95. Jesse's quote below gives rise to the rule.

"There is something that can happen to every athlete and every human being; the instinct to slack off, to give into pain, to give less than your best; the instinct to hope you can win through luck or your opponent not doing his best, instead of going to the limit and past your limit where victory is always found. Defeating those negative instincts that are out to defeat us, is the difference between winning and losing -- and we all face that battle every day."

Stay In Your Lane

The Best Leaders are the Greatest Coaches

Foot Stomper: Perhaps purpose drove Mr. Owens.

Coaching Points

1. Developing a psychological duality is a prerequisite to success.

2. With victory in sight, it is simple to settle for mediocrity.

3. Defeating those negative instincts that are out to defeat us, is the difference between winning and losing -- and we all face that battle every day.

Stay In Your Lane

The Best Leaders are the Greatest Coaches

Chapter Ten

Significance

"There are no medals handed out at the 300-meter mark of the 400-meter dash. To get to significance you must finish the race." Charmas B. Lee

Stay In Your Lane
The Best Leaders are the Greatest Coaches

Andrew Carnegie was an excellent leader and coach. He came to America from his native Scotland when he was a small boy, did various odd jobs, and eventually ended up as the largest steel manufacturer in the United States. At one time, he was the wealthiest man in America. To put his wealth into perspective, he built Pittsburgh's Carnegie Steel Company, which he sold to J. P. Morgan in 1901 for $480 million. Today's equivalent value is nearly $400 billion. He was also a great philanthropist, donating the current equivalent of $79 billion to various charities, universities and libraries. At one point, he had 43 millionaires working for him.

A reporter asked Carnegie how he had hired 43 millionaires. Carnegie responded that those men had not been millionaires when they started working with him, but had become millionaires as a result. The next question was, "How did you develop these men to become so valuable to you that you have paid them so much money?" Carnegie replied, "Men are developed the same way gold is mined. When gold is mined, several tons of dirt must be moved to get an ounce of gold, but one doesn't go into the mine looking for dirt-one goes into the mind looking for gold."

I am able to appreciate Mr. Carnegie's preceding message. With each athlete, great coaches engage in an excavation hoping to uncover the treasure (unique ability) that lies within. Each athlete has their own uniqueness. If we are to bring the sunken treasure to the surface we will need the athlete's full attention. I have watched great coaches help athletes reach incredible heights. I've also had the misfortune of witnessing the well-intended, unknowing coach demoralize an athlete, robbing them of the enriching experience of which they are entitled.

There is no doubt the modern-day athlete (employee) brings a uniquely different set of requirements than in the past and of course that brings with it its own set of challenges. The

Stay In Your Lane
The Best Leaders are the Greatest Coaches

pendulum swings from those who have an inflated sense of entitlement, while others have mastered the "I don't care or poor me attitude." I find that many student athletes lack mental fortitude, and many coaches have no clue how to develop this aspect of the game. Athletes show up disengaged and distracted, which is a challenge to team dynamics. It increases the potential for injury and greatly diminishes the individual or team's chances of achieving the desired outcome. Despite what the student athlete brings to the table it is our responsibility as leaders to solicit the best from them.

Great coaches forge a link between attention and excellence. When I hire a new coach I look for depth, not width. Most are a mile wide in knowledge but only an inch deep in substance. To mine the gold, you must dig through tons of dirt, rocks, mud, etc. As the leader, I have a 100 in 100 out philosophy; the goal is to help every athlete evolve to a place of **SIGNIFICANCE.**

Stay In Your Lane
The Best Leaders are the Greatest Coaches

This is reflective of a young athlete who through some excavation has become a millionaire in her own right. Her millionaire designation is not defined by the size of her 401(k), the type of vehicle she drives or the zip code where she resides. However, if you believe that **people** are the most precious currency then as you read along you will know what I mean.

She currently attends the University of Northern Colorado on athletic scholarship where she is pursuing a degree in Biology. Her goal is to become a marine biologist. Her name is Mackenzie Howie and she will begin her junior year in the fall of 2017. I have known Mackenzie for nine years. She joined Speed T&F in the 7th grade and from the beginning she demonstrated tremendous athletic prowess. She was a dual sport athlete excelling in softball and track. Mack comes from great stock. Dad, now retired, was special forces in the United States Army and mom was a phenomenal high-end competitive swimmer.

After a couple of years of playing both sports, Mack decided to change her goal and focus on the 400-meter hurdles, which in my opinion is the toughest sprint race in the sport of track and field.

Execution of the 400-meter dash without the hurdles takes a high track IQ, preparation, prayer and planning. The following infographic communicates the metaphorical idea of the race phases for the 400-meter dash. The same phases and energy systems are required in the 400-meter hurdles with 10 hurdles set at 30 inches in height strategically placed around the track. The distance from the starting block to the first hurdle is 45 meters. Each hurdle thereafter is 35 meters apart. The race concludes with a brutal 10-meter sprint to the finish. I am getting exhausted just thinking about it.

Stay In Your Lane

The Best Leaders are the Greatest Coaches

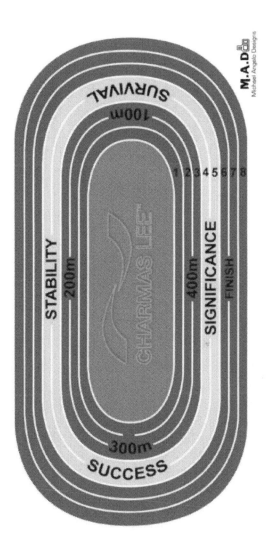

Stay In Your Lane

The Best Leaders are the Greatest Coaches

On average, it takes 500 hours of visualization to master a complex motor skill. These are the four phases of motor skill development.

1. Unconscious Incompetence.

The athlete doesn't know what they don't know.

2. Conscious Incompetence.

Understanding what they don't know and what is required.

3. Conscious Competence.

The athlete excels with an increased measure of confidence.

4. Unconscious Competence.

The athlete is in the zone.

By the end of Mackenzie's junior year in high school she hit phase three (conscious competence). Mackenzie

Stay In Your Lane
The Best Leaders are the Greatest Coaches

attended Pine Creek High School in Colorado Springs, Colorado where she and her teammates experienced an unparalleled spring track and field season. The team established a Colorado State record in the 4x200 meter relay, running a time that was the 6th fastest in the country. They also claimed state titles in the 4x100 and 4x400 meter relays and various other events. Mack and her teammates (smallest school in 5A) amassed a total of 80 points, finishing in 2nd place, just four points behind the unconquerable Fort Collins team (largest school in 5A).

In my opinion, Mackenzie's team is the greatest in school history. Mackenzie continued her quest for athletic excellence that summer and competed at the prestigious National USA Track and Field Junior Olympic Championships which were held in Houston, Texas. During the first round, under the blistering heat of the Texas sun, Mackenzie ran a personal best of 61.02 in the 400-meter hurdles advancing her to the finals. Her time placed her in the top 5% of prep athletes in the country. Mack approached the final round with a laser sharp focus. The starter gave the commands; Runners take

your mark-SET-GO! Mackenzie executed a picture perfect block exit and began her strategic attack with the goal of claiming the 2014 title. When she approached the

5th hurdle the unthinkable happened. A competitor hit a hurdle, sending it flying into Mackenzie's lane. To avoid the flying implement she decelerated and dodged the incoming challenge. This completely disrupted her rhythm which resulted in a 6th place finish. Being a finalist at nationals,

Stay In Your Lane
The Best Leaders are the Greatest Coaches

Mackenzie earned Nike All-America status, however she was extremely disappointed.

During the next winter season Mackenzie had an accident in practice and broke her collar bone. For most, this would have been enough to deter them, but not Mack. Mackenzie recovered from the break and continued to fight the good fight. The trials that Mackenzie experienced introduced her to her strength. Mackenzie is now in the 4th phase (unconscious competence). This summer, while most of her peers are vacationing, Mackenzie is mentoring and coaching athletes at Speed T&F. Each day she moves the dirt, performing the excavation required to fine the gold in these young people's lives. Last year Mackenzie completed her Level I USATF coaching certification and became the first Speed T&F athlete to come back in a "full support" role as a coach. Mackenzie understands the lifetime value of a quality coach and the impact you can make in an athlete's life.

Stay In Your Lane

The Best Leaders are the Greatest Coaches

Mackenzie is my first millionaire. Way to go Mackenzie-Way

to Go!

Mackenzie and Coach Lee, Fall 2015

Stay In Your Lane

The Best Leaders are the Greatest Coaches

Foot Stomper: The lifetime value of a quality leader is priceless.

Coaching Points

1. There are four phases to motor skill (personal-professional) development.

2. It takes 500 hours of visualization to master a complex motor skill.

3. While others were playing, Mackenzie was developing her skills.

4. Her millionaire designation is not defined by the size of her 401(k), the type of vehicle she drives or the zip code where she resides.

Stay In Your Lane

The Best Leaders are the Greatest Coaches

Chapter Eleven

Inspirational to Operational

Stay In Your Lane
The Best Leaders are the Greatest Coaches

Whether I am speaking to a group of athletes, at a conference or at church, my goal is to share something with the audience that will create a life changing dynamic. Motivation without transformation is meaningless. The goal is to move the group from **inspirational to operational.**

Recently I had a meeting with my colleague and good friend Joe Sanders. Joe, a retired colonel, is the former professor and director of the Center for Character and Leadership Development at the United States Air Force Academy. He is currently the Founder and President of Touchstone Leadership Academy, a team of professionals who are committed to creating possibilities for the future.

He is a brilliant man and always shares insightful wisdom. We were having a discussion on vision and he shared something with me that I hadn't heard before. "Charmas," Joe said, "vision is a place to come from not a place to get to." In sharing his perspective, I immediately began to think how I could use this statement in an upcoming presentation.

A place to come from not a place to go to will require an individual to know themselves. I believe that it is important to develop a world class vision because personal excellence is inspired by vision. When we experience setbacks, turbulence, etc. in the form of physical or emotional fatigue those of us with a clear purpose will answer the question with the **vision** we have carefully constructed and will continue to fight. Most people have not identified their **purpose,** do not possess a **vision,** and so they quit when they hit a bump in the road or when the pain kicks in.

Here is a great example. In 1968 in Mexico City, the world's elite runners ran one of history's most grueling marathons. Because of the high altitudes many disheartened world-class athletes quit the race. More than an hour after the gold medal winner had been crowned, the last spectators

Stay In Your Lane
The Best Leaders are the Greatest Coaches

trickled out of the Olympic stadium. As the lights were turned out, a lone Tanzanian runner named John Stephen Akhwari entered the coliseum. As he plodded into view people began to laugh. Laughter turned to silence as the exhausted runner, legs wobbling, right knee wrapped in a now dangling bandage and feet bleeding, slowly moved across the last 400 meters of his race. The stadium lights flashed on as he took his slow painful strides. The crowd that mocked him a few minutes earlier now cheered him on. Others seeing even deeper into the man's spirit began to cry. The crowd was not aware of the collision that took place at the 19 kilometer point of the 42-kilometer race. Athletes were jockeying for position and Akhwari was hit. When he fell he dislocated his knee and jammed his shoulder on the pavement.

Years later sports journalist Bud Greenspan asked this former Olympian, who had become a coach, why he had continued to run the race hours after it became clear he had no chance for a medal. The graying coach replied, "I come from a small, poor country and many people made sacrifices for me to go to Mexico City to run in the marathon. They didn't send me 5000 miles to start the race, they sent me 5000 miles to finish it!"

Stay In Your Lane

The Best Leaders are the Greatest Coaches

Foot Stomper: Vision is a place to come from not a place to get to.

Coaching Points

1. Develop a world class vision because, vision inspires personal excellence.

2. My goal is to move my team from inspirational to operational.

3. Winning is not a sometimes thing, it's an all the time thing.

Stay In Your Lane
The Best Leaders are the Greatest Coaches

About the Author

For more than 29 years. Charmas Lee has been challenging individuals to transform their lives through his dynamic brand of introspection, motivation and personal development. His unique approach to lifelong positive change is cultivated from extensive professional experience building champion athletes at all levels of competition. As a coach, Charmas has developed keen insight into what is necessary to foster a true champion, both on and off the field. He has adapted these insights into a comprehensive strategy that helps individuals, businesses, and corporations reach peak performance.

Charmas holds a Bachelor of Science degree in Organizational Management and many prestigious coaching certifications including USA Track and Field Level 3 Coach; NSCA Certified Strength and Conditioning Specialist; and ACSM Certified Registered Exercise Physiologist. He is one of the elite few in the nation with the certification to coach track and field at the Olympic level. Charmas a proud father of six resides in Colorado Springs with his wife Janice, where he owns three successful businesses specializing in performance and achievement.

To schedule Charmas Lee for a speaking engagement or workshop, visit www.CharmasLee.com or call 719.237.6058.

Stay In Your Lane
The Best Leaders are the Greatest Coaches

Charmas has authored the following books:

Hiding in Plain Sight - Through the sharing of true events, *Hiding in Plain Sight* offers the reader a fresh new perspective on life. Each story is designed to encourage and educate the audience to develop a sense of greater expectations within themselves. *Hiding in Plain Sight* helps us recognize that inspiration is everywhere, that life is a treasure hunt. There is a story within each story that when recognized and applied, will change your trajectory in life. Hiding in Plain Sight communicates a powerful message of awareness and inspiration which helps to remind us that life's true beauty lies in the mind of the beholder. https://www.createspace.com/4061215

A Different Kind of Champion - Will help you gain clarity and focus allowing you to operate at a higher level of awareness and consciousness. As you read these stories and engage in the truth behind each of them, you will find great joy in becoming more of who God has designed you to be. https://www.createspace.com/6092829

Run Your Race - *Run Your Race* is a compilation of select stories from *Hiding in Plain Sight* and *A Different Kind of Champion*. My hope is that as you revisit these stories you will garner new insights, find new inspiration and recommit to running your own metaphorical 400-meter dash with passion, character and conviction. https://www.createspace.com/6529570

REFERENCES

Lee, J., Cohan & Julie Davis-Cohan (2017) *The 5 Coaching Habits of Excellent Leaders*. Cornerstone Leadership

Dungy, Tony with Nathan Whitaker (2009) *Uncommon, Finding Your Path to Significance*. Tyndale House Publishers

Dungy, Tony with Nathan Whitaker (2007) *Quiet Strength, The Principles, Practices & Priorities of Winning in Life*. Tyndale House Publishers

Story of John Stephen Akhwari of Tanzania (2012). June 22, 2017 <http://www.inspiratori.com/sports/story-of-john-steven-aquari-of-tanzania>

Andrew, Paul. July 1, 2017 <http://www.theleadershipcoach.com/2010/burn-your-boats-paul-andrew>

Biography.com Editors. *The Biography.com website* (April 27, 2017) July 18, 2017 <https://www.biography.com/people/jesse-owens-9431142>

Stay In Your Lane
The Best Leaders are the Greatest Coaches

Huddy, John. 'We are all Jews': Israel honors US soldier who stared down Nazi 70 years ago (December 12, 2015) June 29, 2017 <http://www.foxnews.com/world/2015/12/11/first-american-honored-with-holocaust-medal-70-years-later.html>

Blanchard, K., Hersey, P., & Johnson, D. (2001) *Management of Organizational Behavior, Leading Human Resources.* Upper Saddle River, NJ: Prentice Hall

Jr. Lombardi, Vince (2001) *What It Takes To Be #1.* McGraw-Hill, Two Penn Plaza New York, NY.

Covey, S. (1989) *The Seven Habits of Highly Effective People, Powerful Lessons in Personal Change.* New York: Free Press

George, K. (2006) *Coaching Into Greatness, 4 Steps to Success in Business and Life.* Hoboken, NJ: John Wiley & Sons, Inc.

Henschen, K. (2008, Fall). *Psychological Performance Skills.* Coaching Athletics Quarterly. (3), 20-21.

Stay In Your Lane
The Best Leaders are the Greatest Coaches

Loehr, J., & Schwartz, T. (2003) *The Power of Full Engagement, Managing Energy, Not Time, Is the Key to High Performance and Personal Renewal.* New York: The Free Press

Vernacchia, R., McGuire, R. & Cook, D. (1996) *Coaching Mental Excellence: It DOESs matter whether you win or lose.* Portola Valley, CA: Warde Publishers

Vernacchia, R., & Statler, T. (2005) *The Psychology of High-Performance Track and Field.* Mountain View, CA: Track and Field News Press

77942440R00062

Made in the USA
Columbia, SC
06 October 2017